THE SNOW PARTY

DEREK MAHON

THE SNOW PARTY

LONDON
OXFORD UNIVERSITY PRESS
NEW YORK TORONTO
1975

Oxford University Press, Ely House, London W.1

GLASGOW NEW YORK TORONTO MELBOURNE WELLINGTON
CAPE TOWN IBADAN NAIROBI DAR ES SALAAM LUSAKA ADDIS ABABA
DELHI BOMBAY CALCUTTA MADRAS KARACHI LAHORE DACCA
KUALA LUMPUR SINGAPORE HONG KONG TOKYO

ISBN 0 19 211850 1

PR
6063
A34
S6

Printed in Great Britain by
The Bowering Press Limited, Plymouth

For Doreen

Acknowledgements

Acknowledgements are due to the editors of the following, where some of these poems first appeared: *Antaeus, Aquarius, Atlantis, Broadsheet, The Dublin Magazine, Encounter, The Honest Ulsterman, The Irish Times, The Lace Curtain, Lines, The Listener, The Malahat Review, New Irish Writing, The New Review, The New Statesman* and the *TLS*; and to the BBC. A number are included, together with poems from earlier volumes, in *Derek Mahon Reads His Poetry*, issued by Claddagh Records Ltd., Dublin. 'Leaves' was originally published as a poster poem by the Arts Council of Northern Ireland, with art work by Basil Blackshaw. 'The Gipsies' is a version of 'Les Gitans' by Philippe Jaccottet (*Poésie*, Gallimard, 1971). I would like to acknowledge the assistance of the Arts Council of Great Britain.

Contents

Afterlives

for James Simmons

I WAKE in a dark flat
To the soft roar of the world.
Pigeons neck on the white
Roofs as I draw the curtains
And look out over London
Rain-fresh in the morning light.

This is our element, the bright
Reason on which we rely
For the long-term solutions.
The orators yap, and guns
Go off in a back street;
But the faith does not die

That in our time these things
Will amaze the literate children
In their non-sectarian schools
And the dark places be
Ablaze with love and poetry
When the power of good prevails.

What middle-class cunts we are
To imagine for one second
That our privileged ideals
Are divine wisdom, and the dim
Forms that kneel at noon
In the city not ourselves.

I am going home by sea
For the first time in years.
Somebody thumbs a guitar
On the dark deck, while a gull
Dreams at the masthead,
The moon-splashed waves exult.

At dawn the ship trembles, turns
In a wide arc to back
Shuddering up the grey lough
Past lightship and buoy,
Slipway and dry dock
Where a naked bulb burns;

And I step ashore in a fine rain
To a city so changed
By five years of war
I scarcely recognise
The places I grew up in,
The faces that try to explain.

But the hills are still the same
Grey-blue above Belfast.
Perhaps if I'd stayed behind
And lived it bomb by bomb
I might have grown up at last
And learnt what is meant by home.

Leaves

THE prisoners of infinite choice
Have built their house
In a field below the wood
And are at peace.

It is autumn, and dead leaves
On their way to the river
Scratch like birds at the windows
Or tick on the road.

Somewhere there is an afterlife
Of dead leaves,
A stadium filled with an infinite
Rustling and sighing.

Somewhere in the heaven
Of lost futures
The lives we might have led
Have found their own fulfilment.

Homage to Malcolm Lowry

For gear your typewriter and an old rugby-boot,
The voyage started, clearly, when you were born
That danced those empty bottles. When you set out
On a round-the-cosmos trip with the furious Muse
Or lay sweating on a hotel bed in Vera Cruz,
Did you not think you had left that pool astern
Where a soul might bathe and be clean or slake its drought?
In any case, your deportment in those seas
Was faultless. Lighting-blind, you, tempest-torn
At the poles of our condition, did not confuse
The Gates of Ivory with the Gates of Horn.

Going Home

for Douglas Dunn

Wʜʏ we died
Remains a mystery,
One we shall never solve.

The recipes, rhyming slang
And archaic ailments
Of a foreclosed species—

Only a misleading fraction
Will survive on file
To show we could crack a smile.

Only an unrepresentative sample
Will persist on tape
To show what we meant by hope.

Extraordinary people
We were in our time,
How we lived in our time

As if blindfold
Or not wholly serious,
Inventing names for things

To propitiate silence.
It is silence we hug now
In the indigestible

Dawn mist which clings
All afternoon
To the south bank of the Humber—

For ours is the afterlife
Of the unjudgeable,
Of the desolate and free

Who come over
Twice daily from Hull
Disguised as shift workers

And vanish for ever
With a whisper of soles
Under a cindery sky,

The sort of sky
That broke the hearts
Of the foundered legionaries.

Like them we are
Spirits here
With our lunch boxes and

Papers of manumission,
Our speechless debarkations
Without zest or issue.

A pale light wanes
At the pierhead
As if to guide us home

To the blank Elysium
Predicated on our
Eschewal of metaphysics,

A sunken barge rots
In the mud beach
As if finally to discredit

A residual poetry of
Leavetaking and homecoming,
Of work and sentiment;

For this is the last
Homecoming, the end
Of the rainbow—

And the pubs are shut.
There are no
Buses till morning.

The Snow Party

for Louis Asekoff

BASHŌ, coming
To the city of Nagoya,
Is asked to a snow party.

There is a tinkling of china
And tea into china,
There are introductions.

Then everyone
Crowds to the window
To watch the falling snow.

Snow is falling on Nagoya
And farther south
On the tiles of Kyōto.

Eastward, beyond Irago,
It is falling
Like leaves on the cold sea.

Elsewhere they are burning
Witches and heretics
In the boiling squares,

Thousands have died since dawn
In the service
Of barbarous kings—

But there is silence
In the houses of Nagoya
And the hills of Ise.

The Last of the Fire Kings

I WANT to be
Like the man who descends
At two milk churns

With a bulging
String bag and vanishes
Where the lane turns,

Or the man
Who drops at night
From a moving train

And strikes out over the fields
Where fireflies glow
Not knowing a word of the language.

Either way, I am
Through with history—
Who lives by the sword

Dies by the sword.
Last of the fire kings, I shall
Break with tradition and

Die by my own hand
Rather than perpetuate
The barbarous cycle.

Five years I have reigned
During which time
I have lain awake each night

And prowled by day
In the sacred grove
For fear of the usurper,

Perfecting my cold dream
Of a place out of time,
A palace of porcelain

Where the frugivorous
Inheritors recline
In their rich fabrics
Far from the sea.

But the fire-loving
People, rightly perhaps,
Will not countenance this,

Demanding that I inhabit,
Like them, a world of
Sirens, bin-lids
And bricked-up windows—

Not to release them
From the ancient curse
But to die their creature and be thankful.

Thammuz

WHAT will be left
After the twilight of cities,
The flowers of fire,

Will be the soft
Vegetables where our
Politics were conceived.

When we give back
The cleared counties
To the first forest,

The hills to the hills,
The reclaimed
Mudflats to the vigilant sea,

There will be silence, then
A sigh of waking
As from a long dream.

Once more I shall rise early
And plough my country
By first light,

At noon lie down
In a warm field
With the sun on my face,

And after midnight
Fish for stars
In the dark waters.

Once more I shall worship
The moon, make gods
Of clay, gods of stone,

And celebrate
In a world of waste
Their deaths and their return.

Matthew V. 29-30.

LORD, mine eye offended
So I plucked it out.
Imagine my chagrin

When the offence continued.
So I plucked out
The other but

The offence continued.
In the dark now and
Working by touch, I shaved

My head, the offence continued.
Removed an ear,
Another, dispatched the nose,

The offence continued.
Imagine my chagrin.
Next, in long strips, the skin—

Razored the tongue, the toes,
The personal nitty-gritty.
The offence continued.

But now, the thing
Finding its own momentum,
The more so since

The offence continued,
I entered upon
A prolonged course

Of lobotomy and vivisection,
Reducing the self
To a rubble of organs,

A wreckage of bones
In the midst of which, somewhere,
The offence continued.

Quicklime, then, for the
Calcium, paraquat
For the unregenerate offal,

A spreading of topsoil,
A ploughing of this
And a sowing of it with barley.

Paraffin for the records
Of birth, flu
And abortive scholarship,

For the whimsical postcards,
The cheques
Dancing like hail,

The surviving copies
Of poems published
And unpublished. A scalpel

For the casual turns
Of phrase engraved
On the minds of others,

A chemical spray
For the stray
Thoughts hanging in air,

For the people
Who breathed them in.
Sadly, therefore, deletion

Of the many people
From their desks, beds,
Breakfasts, buses,

Pick-ups and catamarans.
Deletion of their
Machinery and architecture,

All evidence whatever
Of civility and reflection,
Of laughter and tears.

Destruction of all things on which
That reflection fed,
Of vegetable and bird,

Erosion of all rocks
From the holiest mountain
To the least stone,

Evaporation of all seas,
The extinction of heavenly bodies—
Until, at last, offence

Was not to be found
In that silence without bound.
Only then was I fit for human society.

The Antigone Riddle

ELOCUTION, logic, political science,
Antibiotics, do-it-yourself,
And a plover flops in his oil slick.

Shy minerals contract at the sound of his voice,
Cod point in silence when his bombers pass,
And the windfall waits
In silence for his departure
Before it drops in
Silence to the long grass.

The North African Campaign

I was here before but I lost last time.
A light wind touches the dust
Of my confidence and dismay
And is almost like voices.
Stout lads, they are at peace now
In the heaven of the Carthaginians,
Watching the contemporary
Elephants at work on the holy places.

Cavafy

1 *The City*

To have gone to a new country, a new sea,
Another, finer city—
Too late now to deliver
The condemned heart from the vicinity
Of lost chances, dead ends,
Dark ruins of the life
You have wasted here.

There is no new country, no new sea.
Only the same old city
Shadows you night and day.
You will spend your life
In the same dim suburb,
In the same house grow grey.

In this city of homecomings
Where all voyages end
There is no way out.
Your failure here
Was a failure everywhere
In the world at large, as if talked about.

2 *Voices*

Definitive voices of the loved dead
Or the loved lost, as good as dead,
Speak to us in our dreams
Or at odd moments.

Listening, we hear again,
Like music at night,
The original poetry of our lives.

3 *A Considered Pause*

When the time comes to decide
The man who will say yes
Does so without hesitation
And the future is his;
While the hesitation
Of the man who says no
Is a considered pause, as if
He has known all along
There was no future in it.

4 *The Souls of the Old Men*

The souls of the old men
Cling to their bodies
With fierce loyalty, with love
Born of necessity—
Where else could they live?

Gazing from behind clouded eyes
They are tired
Of the old habitations,

Resentful of their own
Impatience to be gone.

5 *The Facts of Life*

I will not be known by what I did or said.
The facts of life conspired
To block action, tie tongue. Nothing
Came out as I intended.

No, look for my secret
In the lost grin,
The poker-faced elision.

Reborn in the ideal society
I shall act and speak
With a freedom denied me
By the life we know.

Dead of Night

WAKING at dead of night I remembered that
I was in Spain, and lay listening to a dog bark
in the dark country—with the starlit stones,
the reflective spider,

the grapes dreaming of the days of wine.

The chair squeaks . . .

THE chair squeaks in a high wind,
Rain falls from its branches,
The kettle yearns for the
Mountain, the soap for the sea.
In a tiny stone church
On the desolate headland
A lost tribe is singing abide with me.

After Nerval

YOUR great mistake is to disregard the satire
Bandied among the mute phenomena.
Be strong if you must, your brusque hegemony
Means fuck-all to the somnolent sun-flower
Or the extinct volcano. What do you know
Of the revolutionary theories advanced
By turnips, or the sex-life of cutlery?
Everything is susceptible, Pythagoras said so.

An ordinary common-or-garden brick wall, the kind
For talking to or banging your head on,
Resents your politics and bad draughtsmanship.
God is alive and lives under a stone.
Already in a lost hub-cap is conceived
The ideal society which will replace our own.

The Gipsies

THERE are fires under the trees.
Low voices speak to the sleeping nations
From the fringes of cities.

If, shortlived souls that we are,
We pass silently
On the dark road tonight,
It is for fear you should die,
Perpetual murmur
Around the hidden light.

The Window

```
woodwoodwoodwoodwoodwoodwoodwood
io                              oo
n o                            o w
d   d                          w   i
o   w                          o   n
w   o                          o   d
i   o                          d   o
n   d                          w   w
d   w                          o   i
o   o                          o   n
w   o                          d   d
i   d                          w   o
n   w            wind          o   w
d   o                          o   i
o   o                          d   n
w   d                          w   d
i   w                          o   o
n   d                          w   w
d o                              o i
oo                               on
woodwoodwoodwoodwoodwoodwoodwood
dwoodwoodwoodwoodwoodwoodwoodwoodw
odwoodwoodwoodwoodwoodwoodwoodwoodwo
```

A Hermit

I HAVE abandoned the dream kitchens for a low fire and a prescriptive literature of the spirit. A storm snores on the desolate sea. The nearest shop is four miles away. When I walk there through the shambles of the morning for tea and firelighters, the mountain paces me in a snow-lit silence. My days are spent in conversation with stags and blackbirds; at night fox and badger gather at my door. I have stood for hours watching a salmon doze in the tea-gold dark, for weeks watching a spider weave in a pale light, for months listening to the sob story of a stone on the road—the best, most monotonous sob story I have ever heard.

I am an expert on frost crystals and the silence of crickets, a confidant of the stinking shore, the stars in the mud. There is an immanence in these things which drives me, despite my scepticism, almost to the point of speech. Like sunlight cleaving the lake mist at morning, or when tepid water runs cold at last from the tap. I have been working for years on a four-line poem about the life of a leaf. I think it may come out right this winter.

The Apotheosis of Tins

HAVING spent the night in a sewer of precognition, consoled by moon-glow, air-chuckle, and the retarded pathos of mackerel, we wake among shoelaces and white wood to a raw wind and the cries of gulls. Deprived of use, we are safe now from the historical nightmare, and may give our attention at last to things of the spirit, noticing for example the consanguinity of sand and stone, how they are thicker than water. This is the terminal democracy of hatbox and crab, of hock and Windowlene. It is always rush hour. If we have learnt one thing from our desertion by the sour smudge on the horizon, from the erosion of labels, it is the value of self-definition. No-one, not even the pensioner whose shadow strains above us after dawn and before dusk, will have our trust. We resist your patronage, your reflective leisure.

Promoted artifacts by the dereliction of our creator, and greater now than the sum of his skills, we shall be with you while there are beaches. Imperishable by-products of the perishable will, we shall lie like skulls in the hands of soliloquists. The longest queues in the science museum will form at our last homes saying, think now, what an organic relation of art to life in the dawn of time, what saintly devotion to the notion of permanence in the flux of sensation and crisis, perhaps we can learn from them.

Epitaph for Flann O'Brien

WITHOUT whiskey, without porter
Of the black porter-blackness
And wine in fine bottles
Have I been these nine years.

Far have I travelled—
To Moyle and Clonmacnoise,
To Glen Etive and Parnell Square.
My feet are killing me.

Death is no bed of roses,
Wild dogs would not be in it.
The north wind has chilled my manhood,
Jesus Christ it is desperate.

Badgers, hares my bedfellows,
The black earth my earth-bed—
Not much here to write home about.
Give us a sup of that.

September in Great Yarmouth

THE woodwind whistles down the shore
Piping the stragglers home; the gulls
Snaffle and bolt their final mouthfuls.
Only the youngsters call for more.

Chimneys breathe and beaches empty,
Everyone queues for the inland cold—
Middle-aged parents growing old
And teenage kids becoming twenty.

Now the first few spots of rain
Spatter the sports-page in the gutter.
Council workmen stab the litter.
You have sown and reaped, now sow again.

The band packs in, the banners drop,
The ice-cream stiffens in its cone,
The boatman lifts his megaphone—
Come in, fifteen, your time is up.

The Banished Gods

The old gods of the rain lie wrapped in pools.

Hart Crane, *The Bridge*

Delos, far-shining star of dark-blue earth,
　Reverts to the sea its mother.
　　The tiny particles,
　Rose, quartz and amethyst,
Panic into the warm brine together.

Near the headwaters of the longest river
　There is a forest clearing,
　　A dank, misty place
　Where light stands in columns
And birds sing with a noise like paper tearing.

Far from land, far from the trade routes,
　In an unbroken dream-time
　　Of penguin and whale
　The seas sigh to themselves
Reliving the days before the days of sail.

Down a dark lane at the arse-end of nowhere
　A farm dog lies by a dead fire
　　Dreaming of nothing
　While a window turns slowly grey
Brightening a laid table and hung clothing.

Where the wires end the moor seethes in silence,
　Scattered with scree, primroses,
　　Feathers and faeces.
　It shelters the hawk and hears
In dreams the forlorn cries of lost species.

It is here that the banished gods are in hiding,
    Here they sit out the centuries
        In stone, water
        And the hearts of trees,
    Lost in a reverie of their own natures—

Of zero-growth economics and seasonal change
    In a world without cars, computers
        Or chemical skies,
    Where thought is a fondling of stones
And wisdom a five-minute silence at moonrise.

A Refusal to Mourn

for Maurice Leitch

He lived in a small farmhouse
At the edge of a new estate.
The trim gardens crept
To his door, and car engines
Woke him before dawn
On dark winter mornings.

All day there was silence
In the bright house. The clock
Ticked on the kitchen shelf,
Cinders moved in the grate
And a warm briar gurgled
When the old man talked to himself;

But the doorbell seldom rang
After the milkman went,
And if a coat-hanger
Knocked in an open wardrobe
That was a great event
To be pondered on for hours

While the wind thrashed about
In the back garden, raking
The roof of the hen-house,
And swept clouds and gulls
Eastwards over the lough
With its flap of tiny sails.

Once a week he would visit
An old shipyard crony,
Inching down to the road
And the blue country bus
To sit and watch sun-dappled
Branches whacking the windows

While the long evening shed
Weak light in his empty house,
On the photographs of his dead
Wife and their six children
And the Missions to Seamen angel
In flight above the bed.

'I'm not long for this world'
Said he on our last evening,
'I'll not last the winter',
And grinned, straining to hear
Whatever reply I made;
And died the following year.

In time the astringent rain
Of those parts will clean
The words from his gravestone
In the crowded cemetery
That overlooks the sea
And his name be mud once again

And his boilers lie like tombs
In the mud of the sea-bed
Till the next ice-age comes
And the earth he inherited
Is gone like Neanderthal Man
And no records remain.

But the secret bred in the bone
On the dawn strand survives
In other times and lives,
Persisting for the unborn
Like a claw-print in concrete
After the bird has flown.

Flying

A WAND of sunlight
Touches the rush hour
Like the finger of heaven.

A land of cumulus
Seen from above
Is the life to come.

A Disused Shed in Co. Wexford

Let them not forget us, the weak souls among the asphodels.
Seferis, Mythistorema

for J. G. Farrell

EVEN now there are places where a thought might grow—
Peruvian mines, worked out and abandoned
To a slow clock of condensation,
An echo trapped for ever, and a flutter of
Wildflowers in the lift-shaft,
Indian compounds where the wind dances
And a door bangs with diminished confidence,
Lime crevices behind rippling rainbarrels,
Dog corners for shit burials;
And in a disused shed in Co. Wexford,

Deep in the grounds of a burnt-out hotel,
Among the bathtubs and the washbasins
A thousand mushrooms crowd to a keyhole.
This is the one star in their firmament
Or frames a star within a star.
What should they do there but desire?
So many days beyond the rhododendrons
With the world waltzing in its bowl of cloud,
They have learnt patience and silence
Listening to the crows querulous in the high wood.

They have been waiting for us in a foetor of
Vegetable sweat since civil war days,
Since the gravel-crunching, interminable departure
Of the expropriated mycologist.

He never came back, and light since then
Is a keyhole rusting gently after rain.
Spiders have spun, flies dusted to mildew,
And once a day, perhaps, they have heard something—
A trickle of masonry, a shout from the blue
Or a lorry changing gear at the end of the lane.

There have been deaths, the pale flesh flaking
Into the earth that nourished it;
And nightmares, born of these and the grim
Dominion of stale air and rank moisture.
Those nearest the door grow strong—
Elbow room! Elbow room!
The rest, dim in a twilight of crumbling
Utensils and broken pitchers, groaning
For their deliverance, have been so long
Expectant that there is left only the posture.

A half century, without visitors, in the dark—
Poor preparation for the cracking lock
And creak of hinges. Magi, moonmen,
Powdery prisoners of the old regime,
Web-throated, stalked like triffids, racked by drouth
And insomnia, only the ghost of a scream
At the flash-bulb firing squad we wake them with
Shows there is life yet in their feverish forms.
Grown beyond nature now, soft food for worms,
They lift frail heads in gravity and good faith.

They are begging us, you see, in their wordless way,
To do something, to speak on their behalf
Or at least not to close the door again.
Lost people of Treblinka and Pompeii!
Save us, save us, they seem to say,

Let the god not abandon us
Who have come so far in darkness and in pain.
We too had our lives to live.
You with your light meter and relaxed itinerary,
Let not our naive labours have been in vain!